Mazes

for Preschool Kids

100 Easy Mazes for Kids Ages 5-6

1

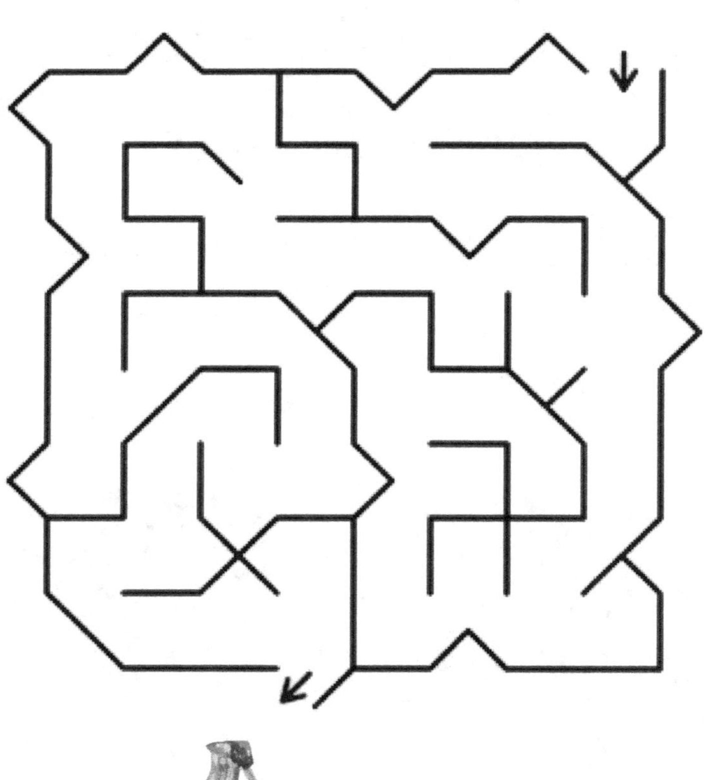

2

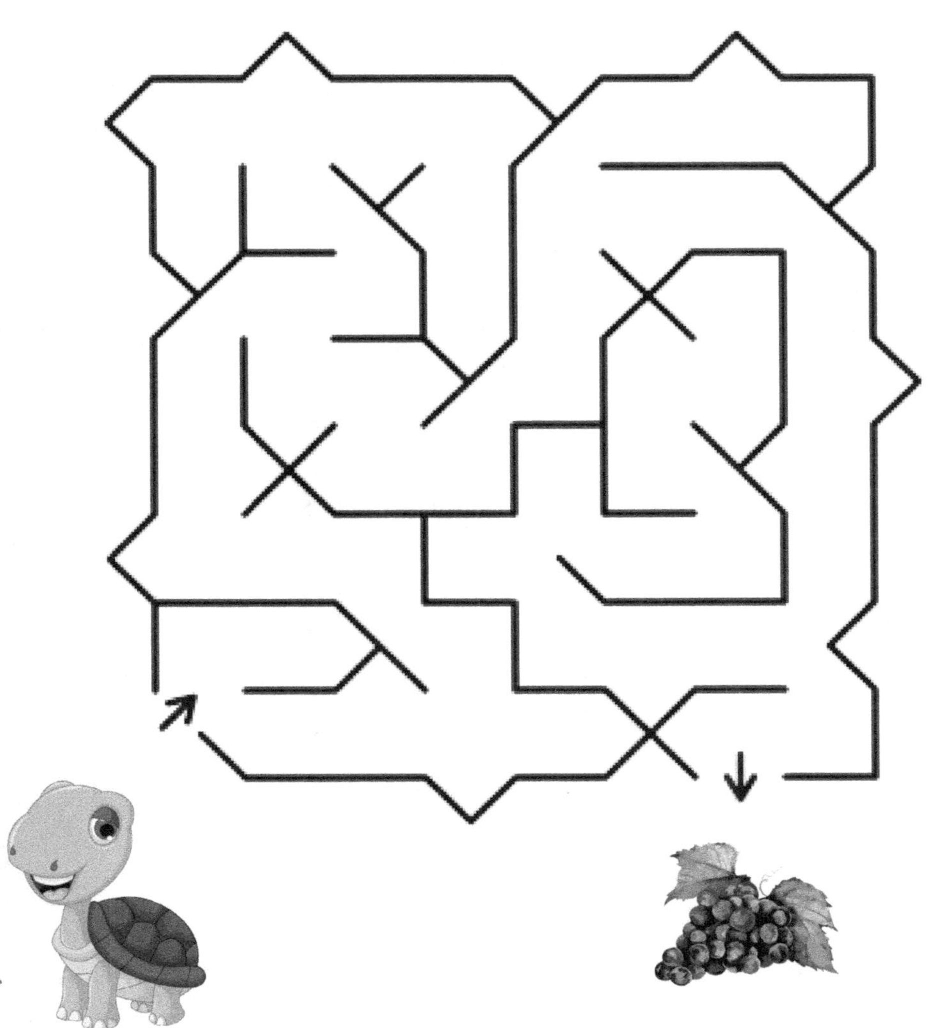

3

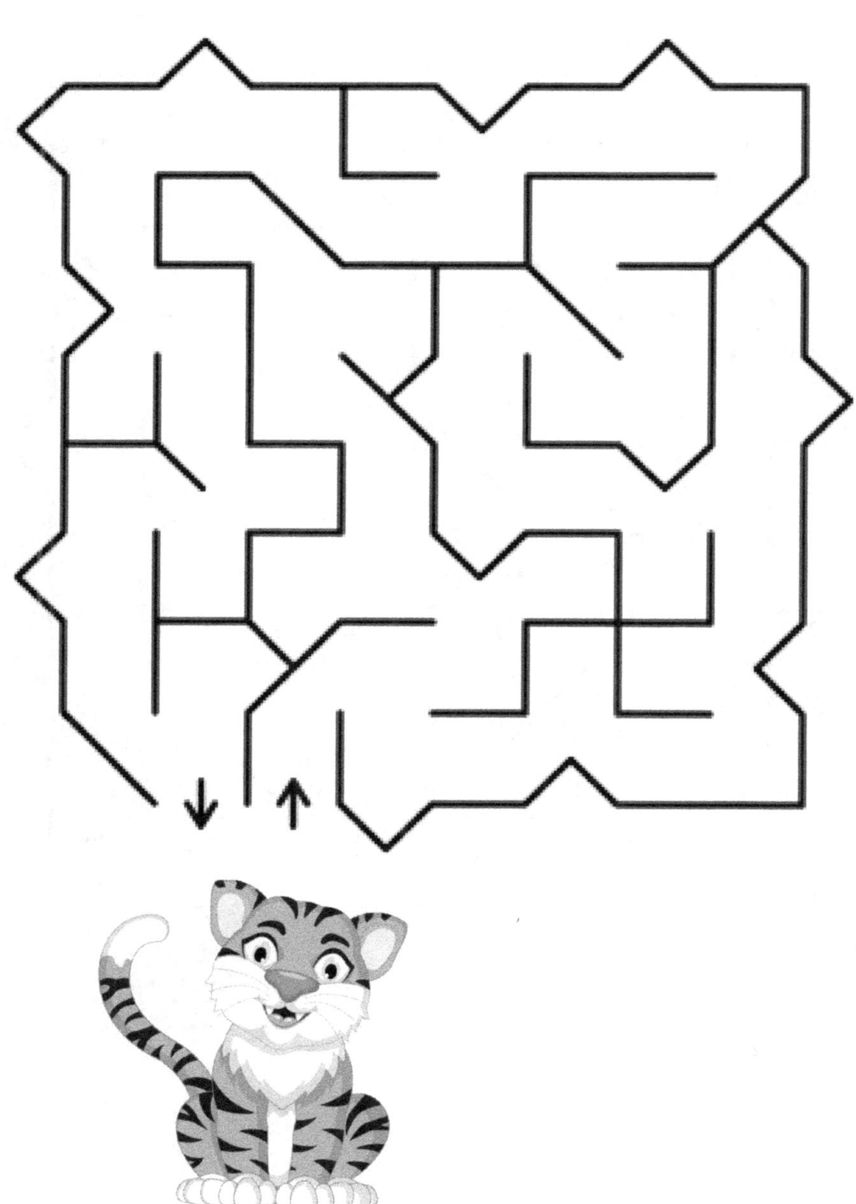

4

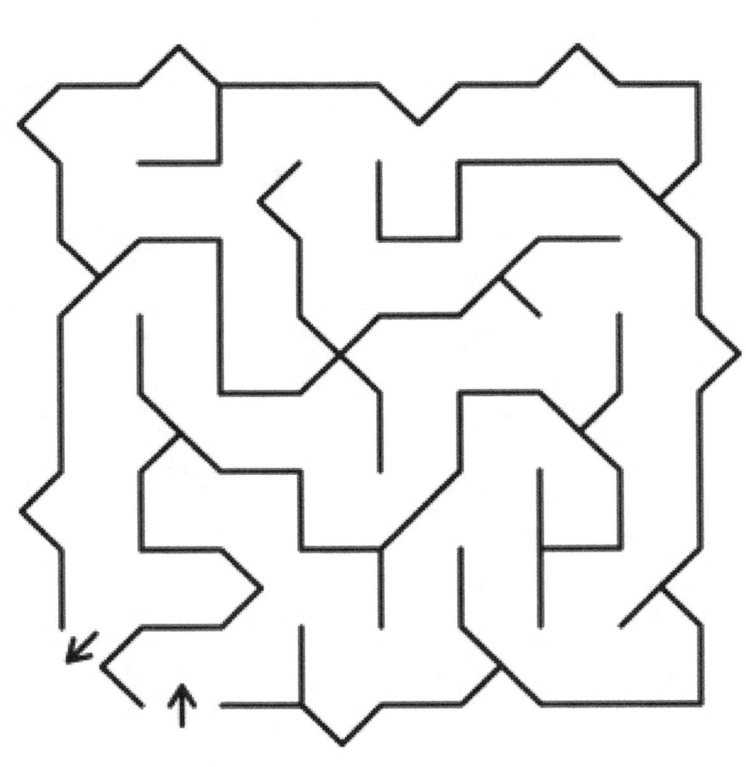

5

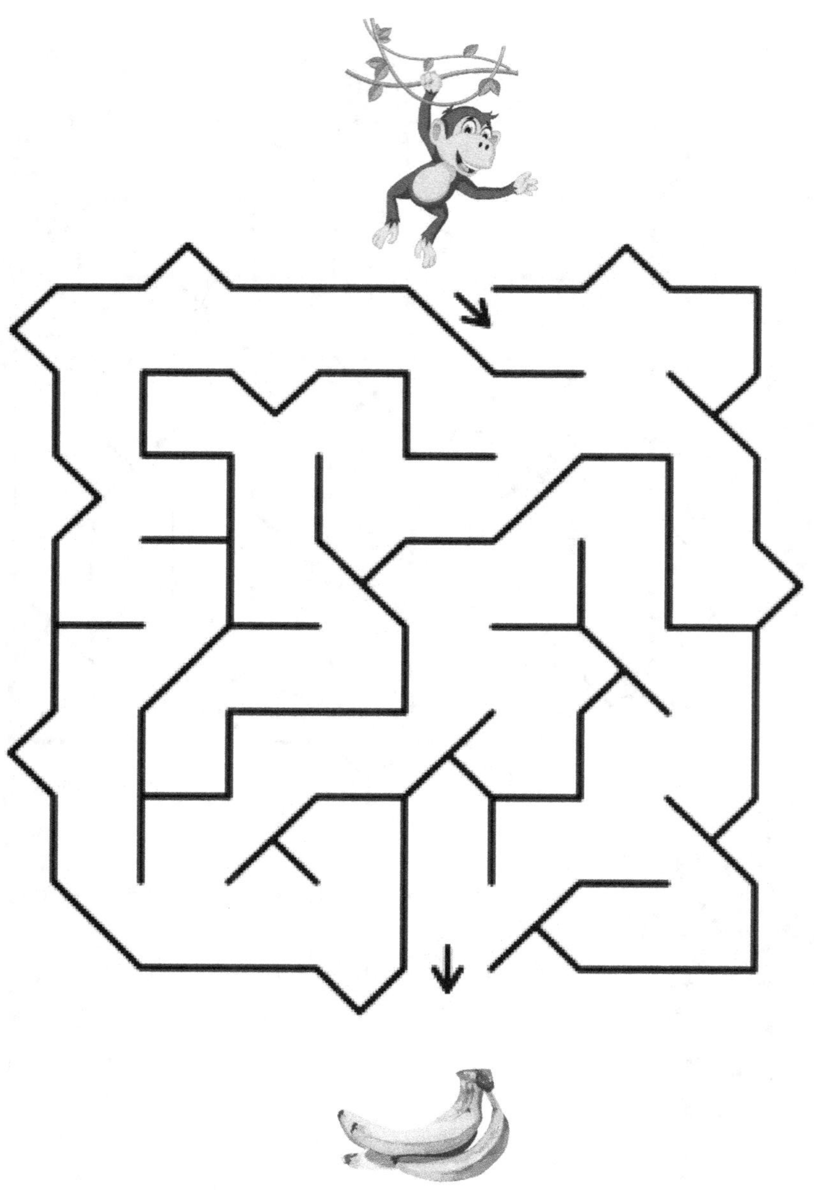

6

7

8

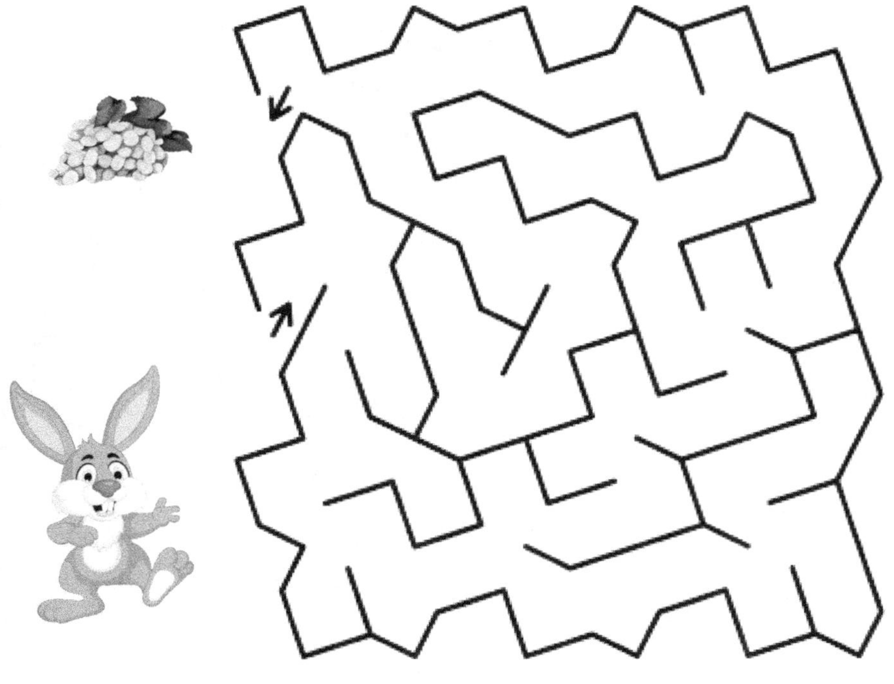

9

10

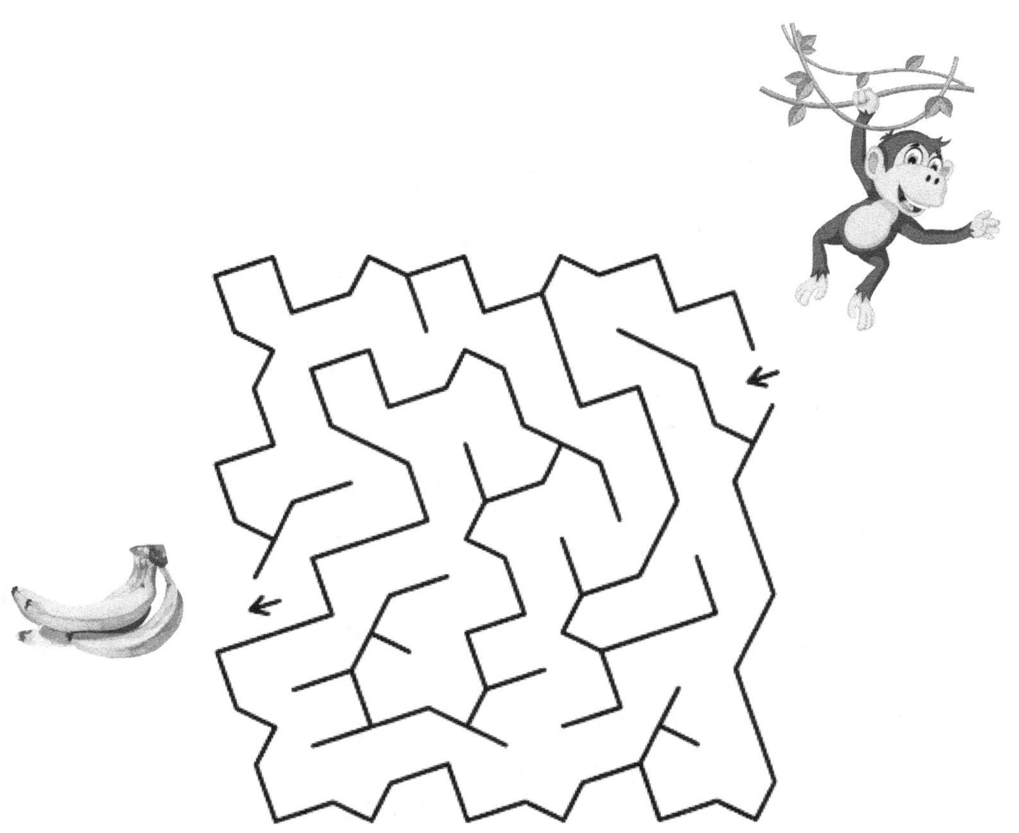

11

12

13

14

15

16

17

18

19

20

21

22

23

24

25

26

27

28

29

30

31

32

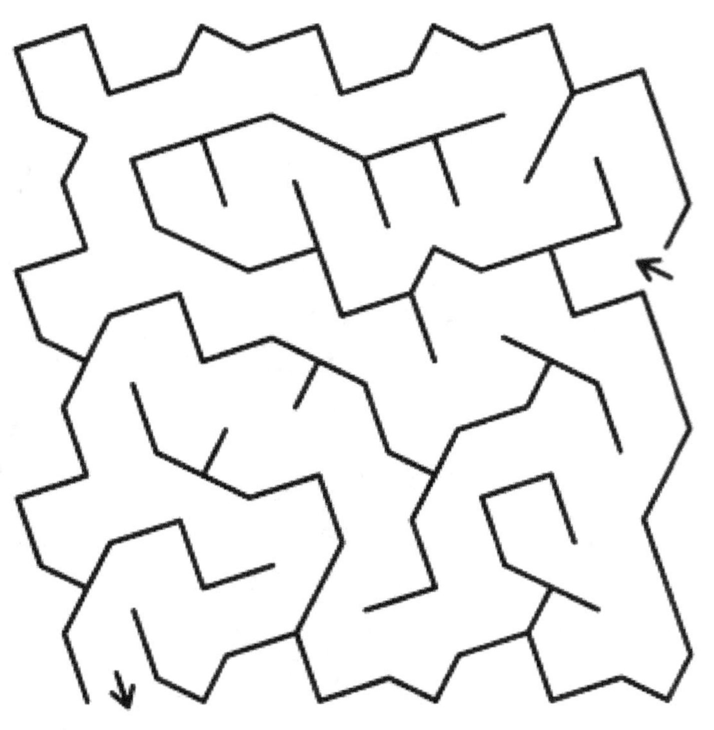

33

34

35

36

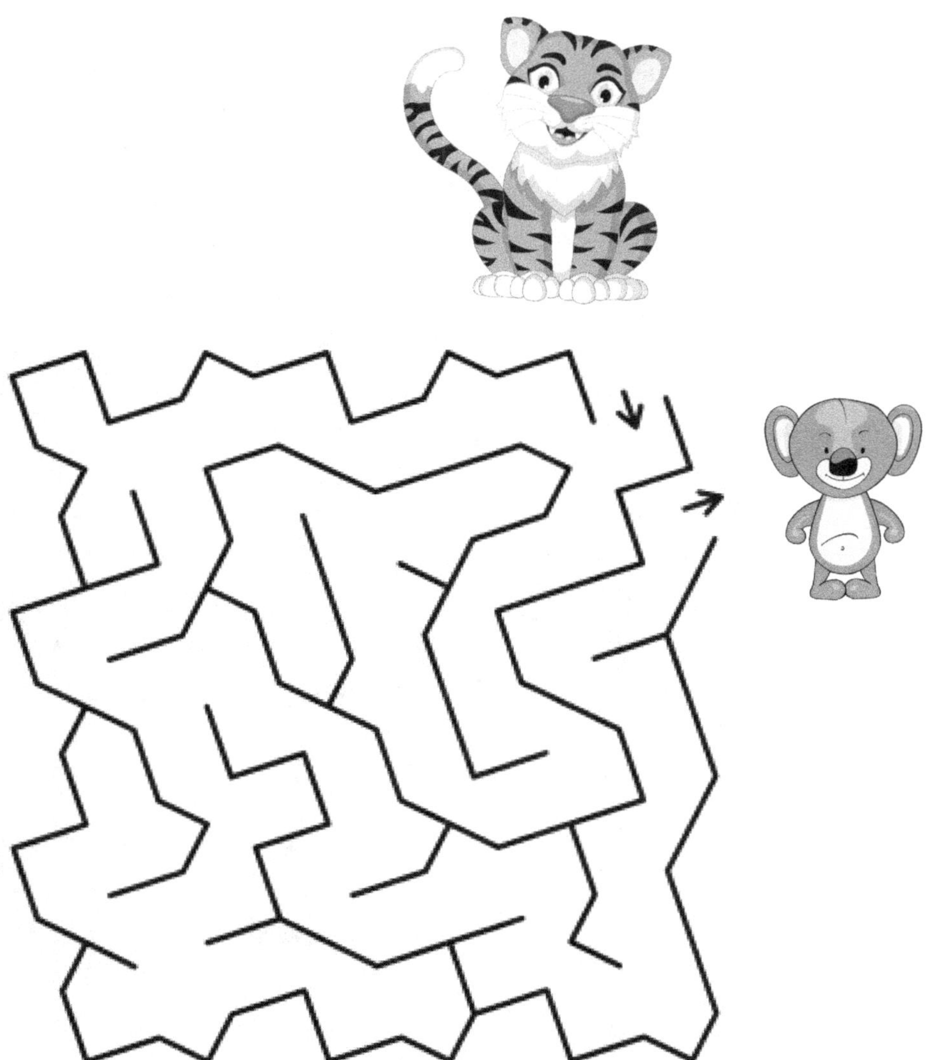

37

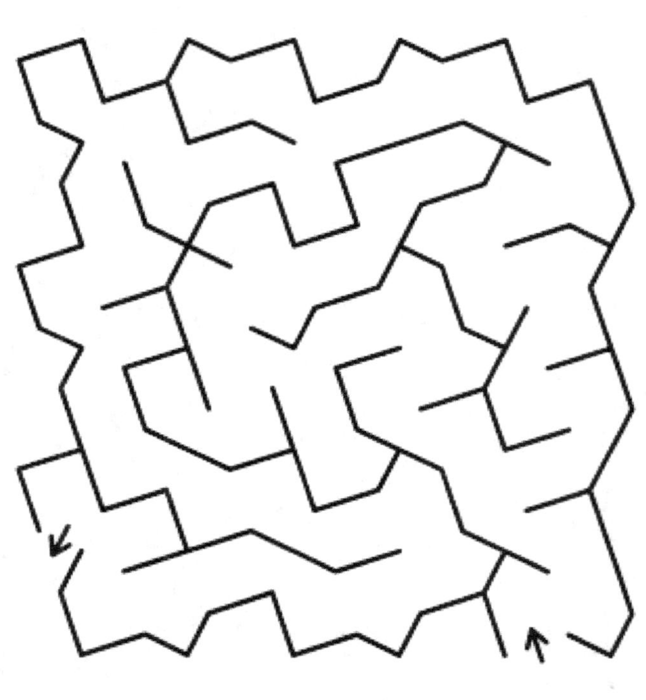

38

39

40

41

42

43

44

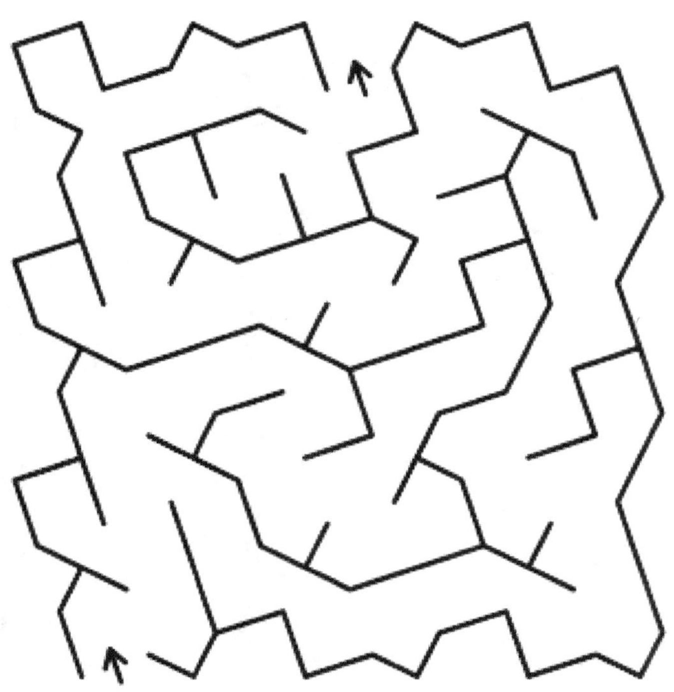

45

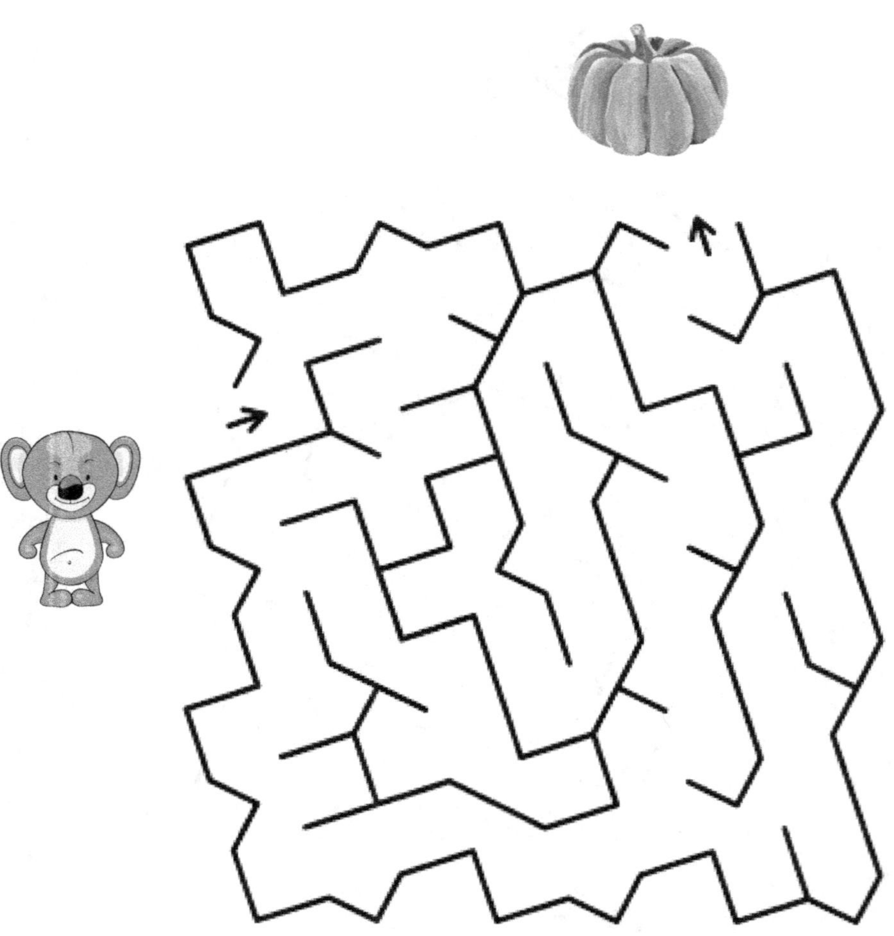

46

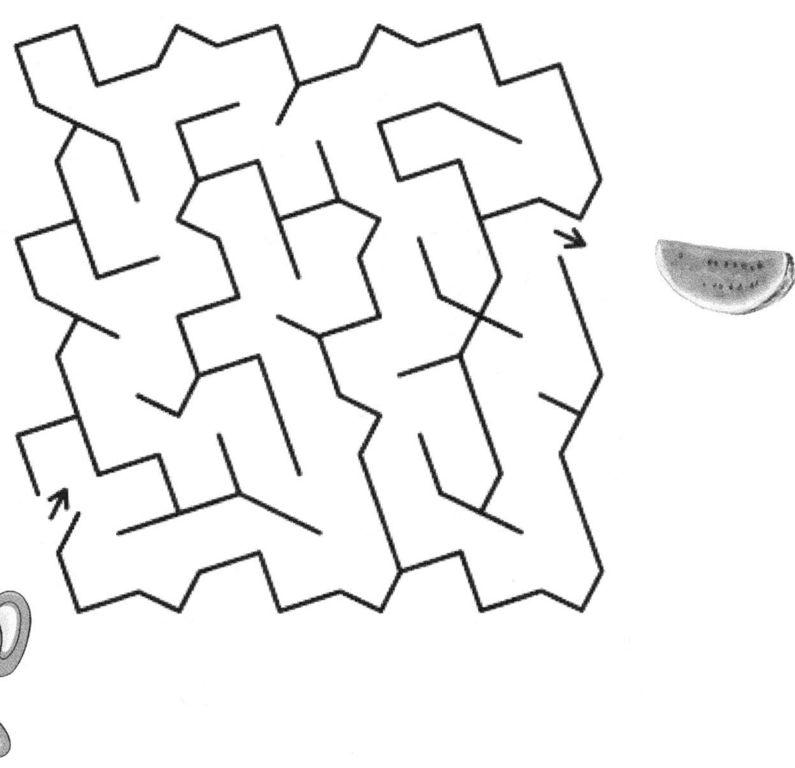

47

48

49

50

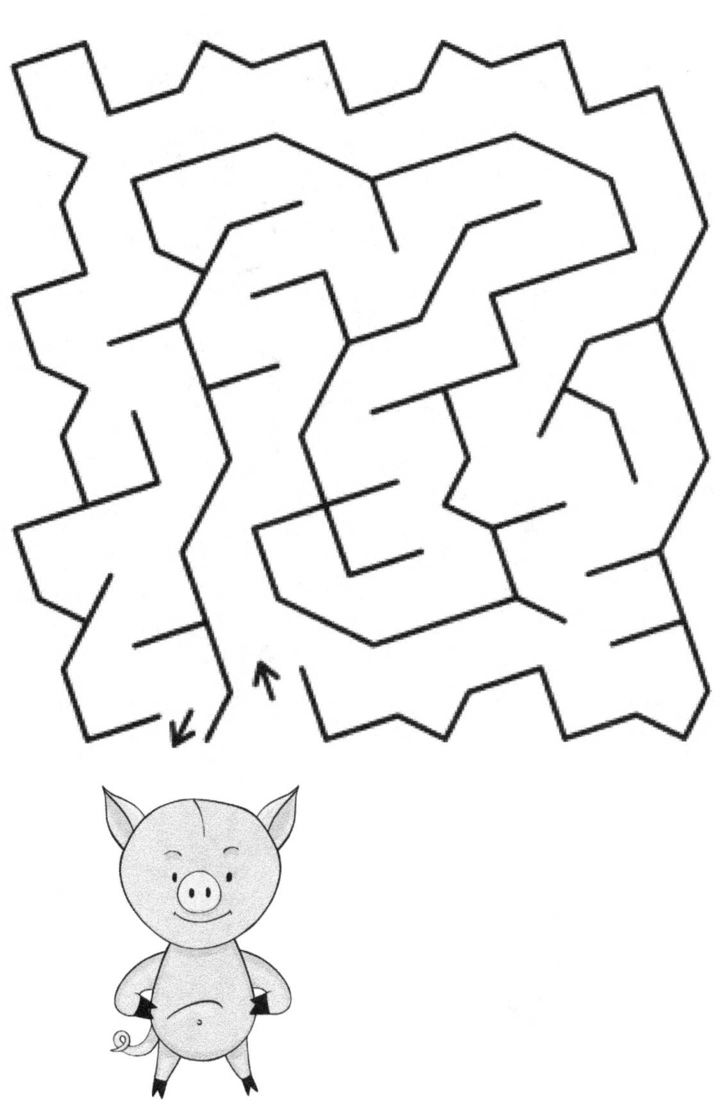

51

52

53

54

55

56

57

58

59

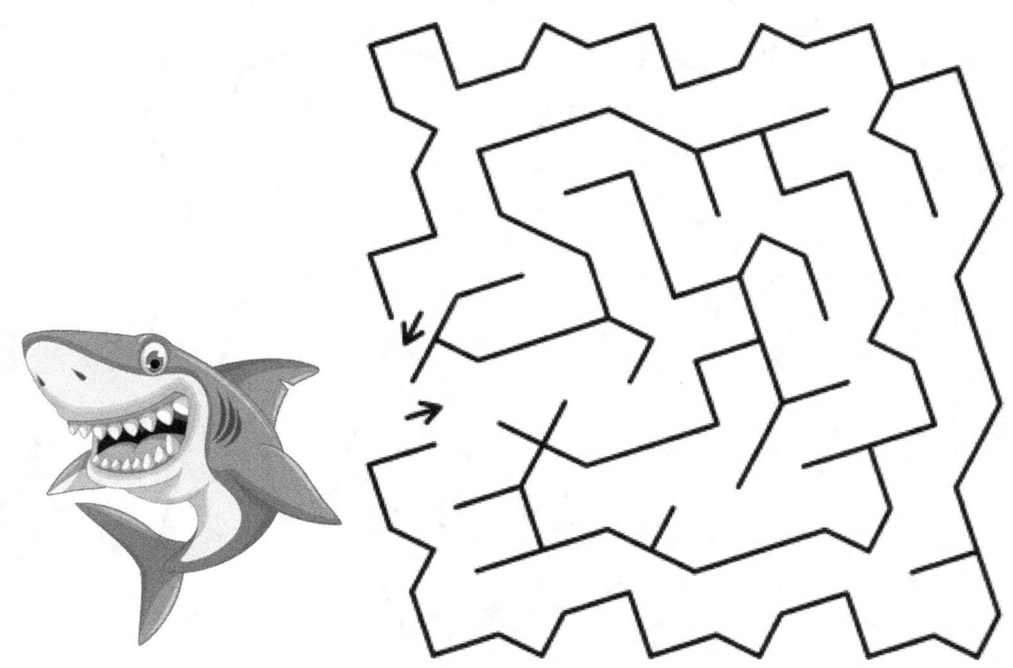

60

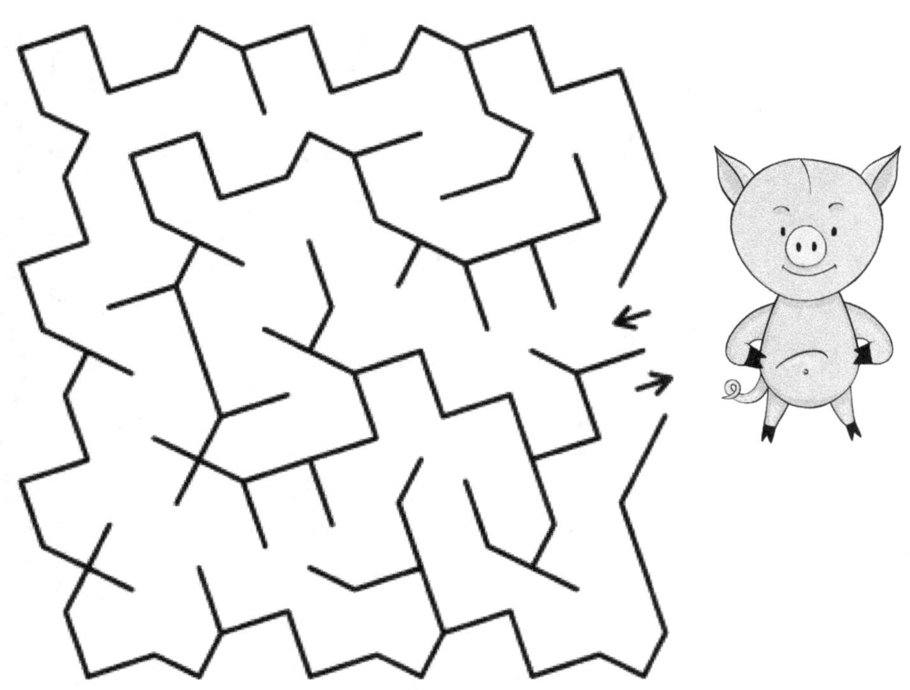

61

62

63

64

65

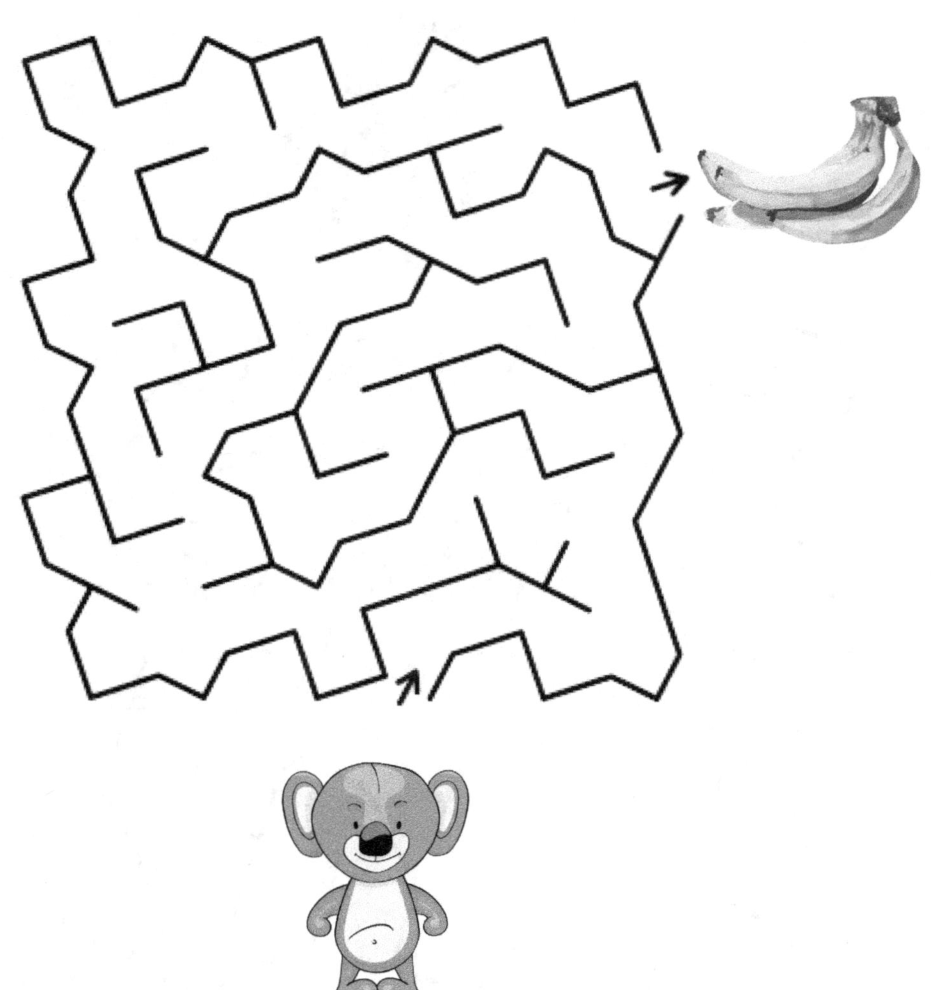

66

67

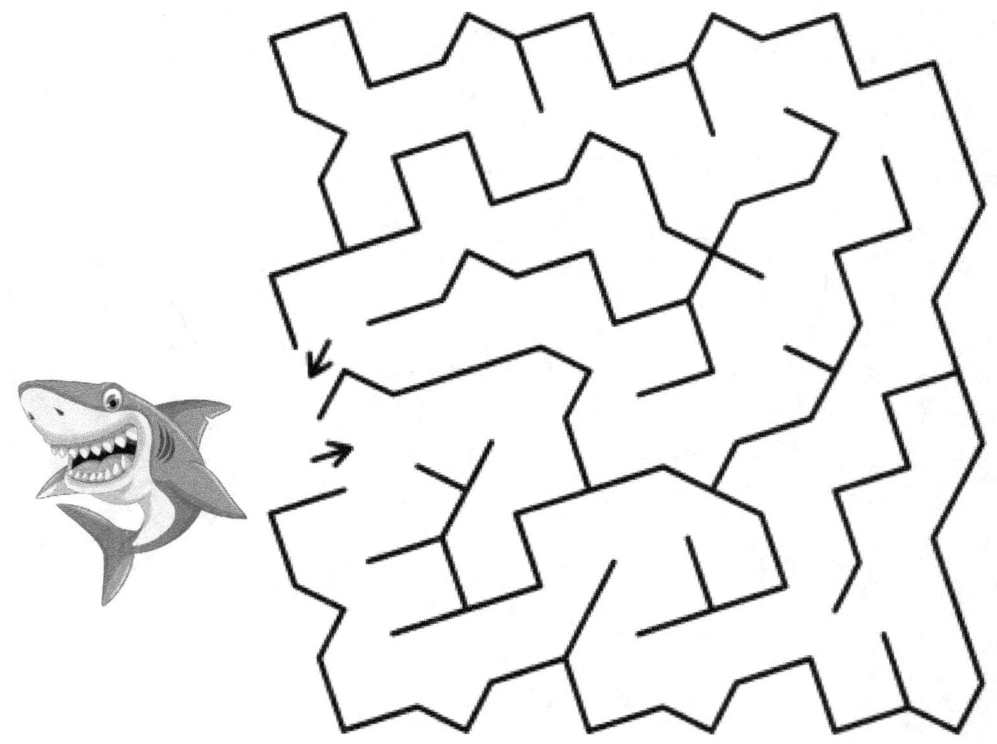

68

69

70

71

72

73

74

75

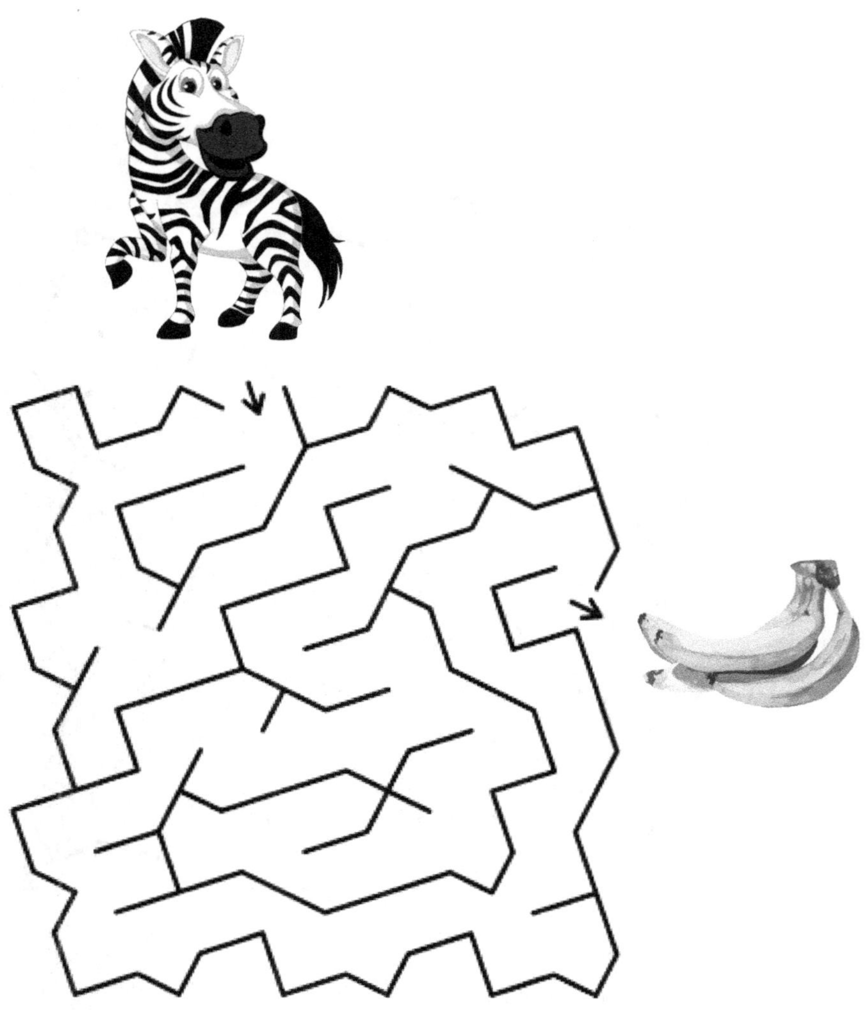

76

77

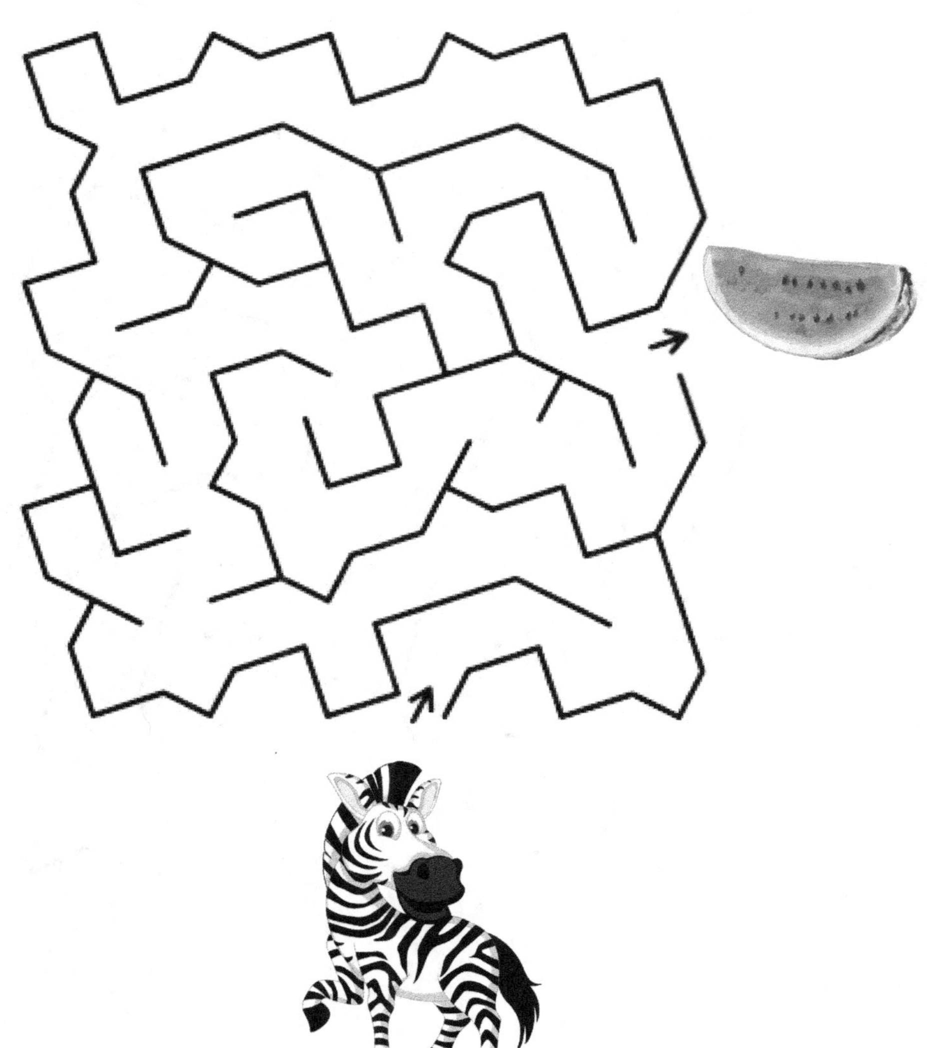

78

79

80

81

82

83

84

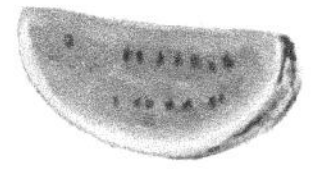

85

87

88

89

90

91

92

93

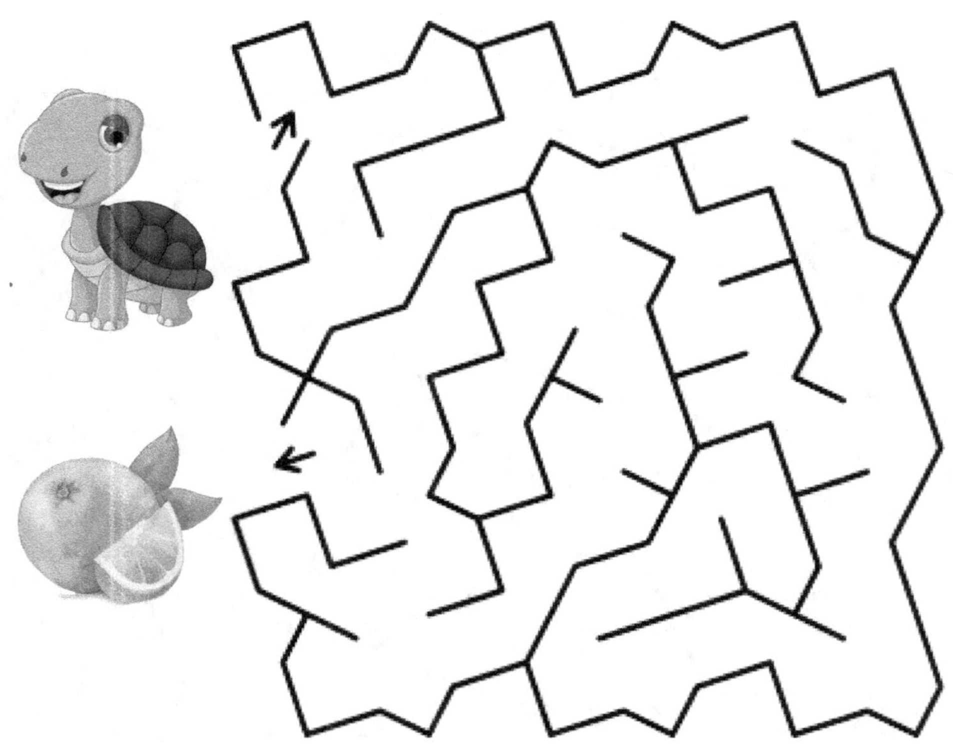

94

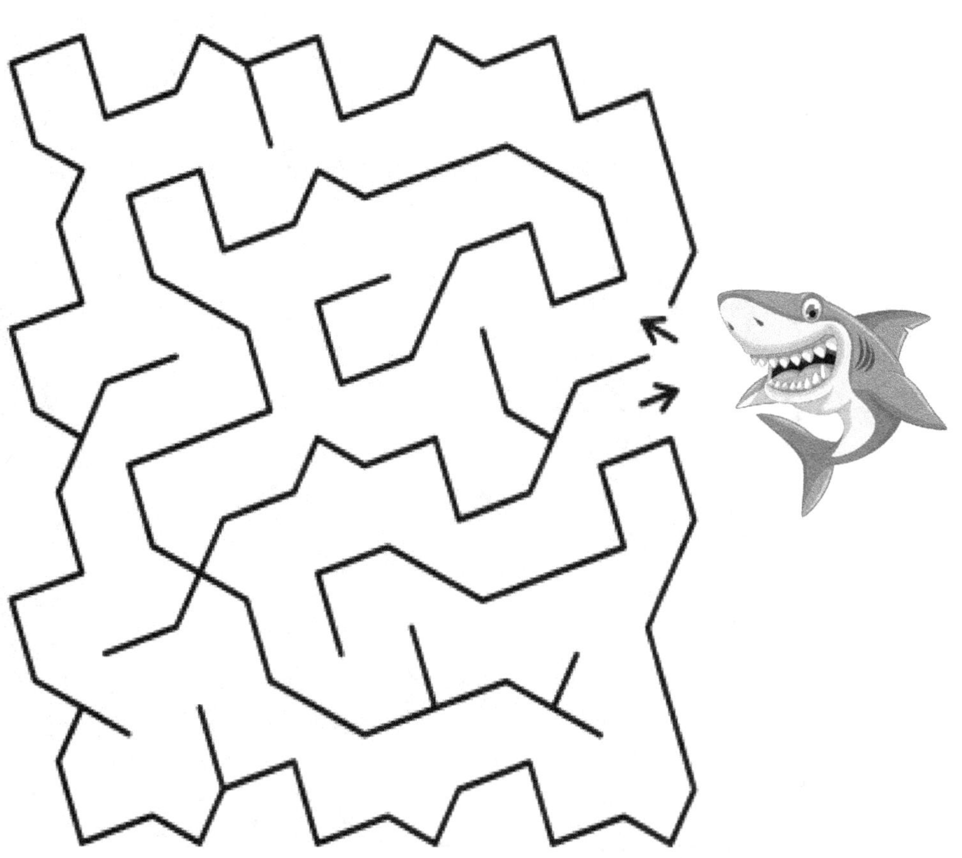

95

96

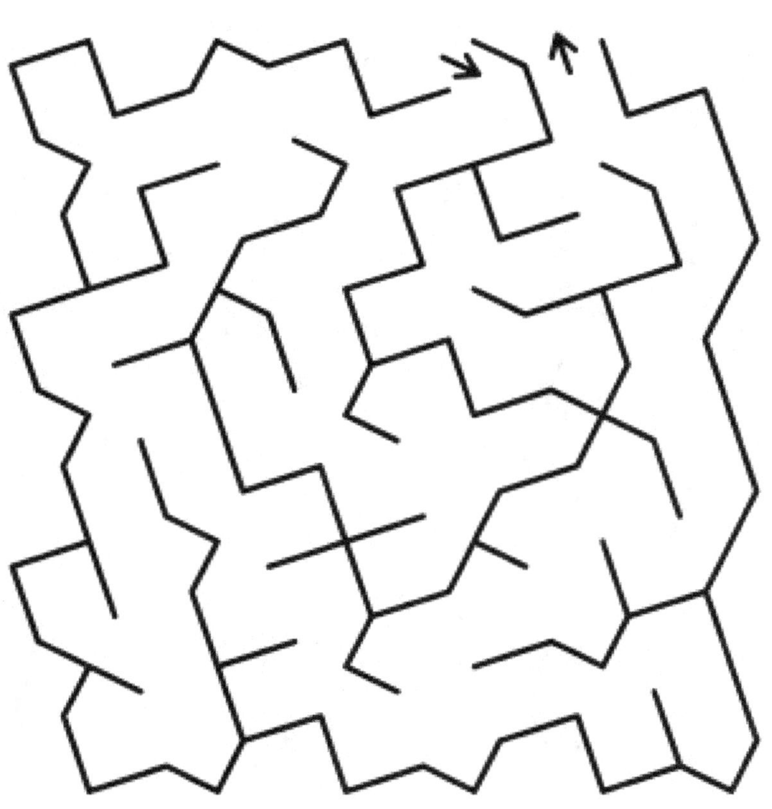

97

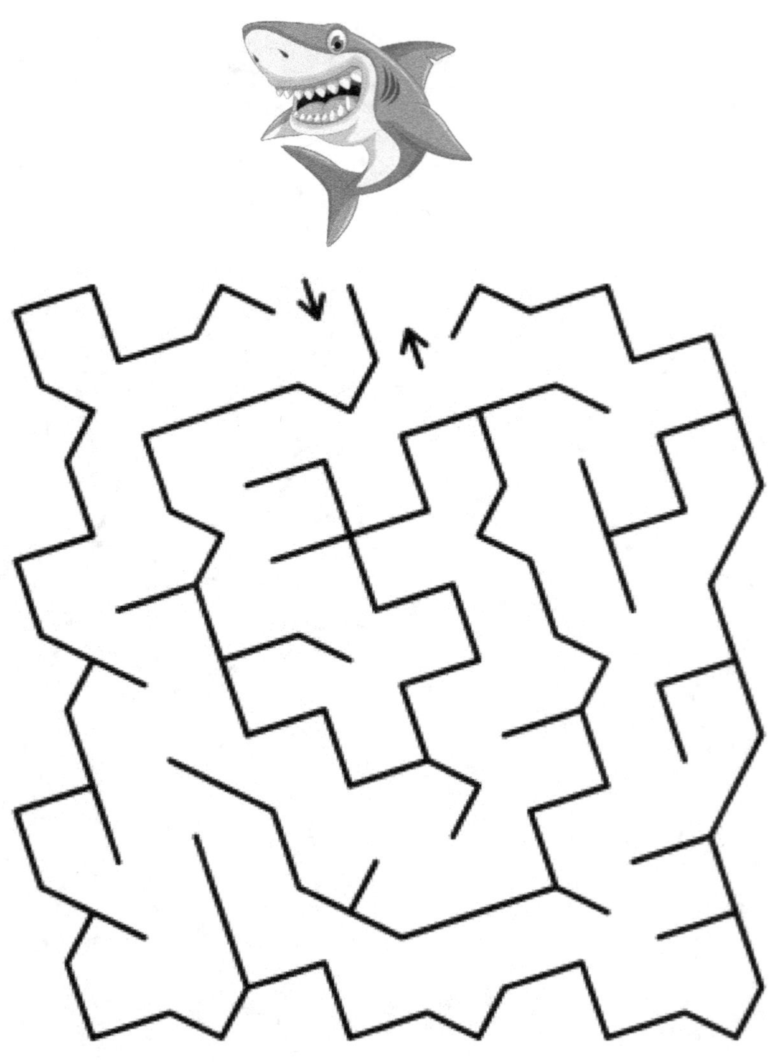

98

99

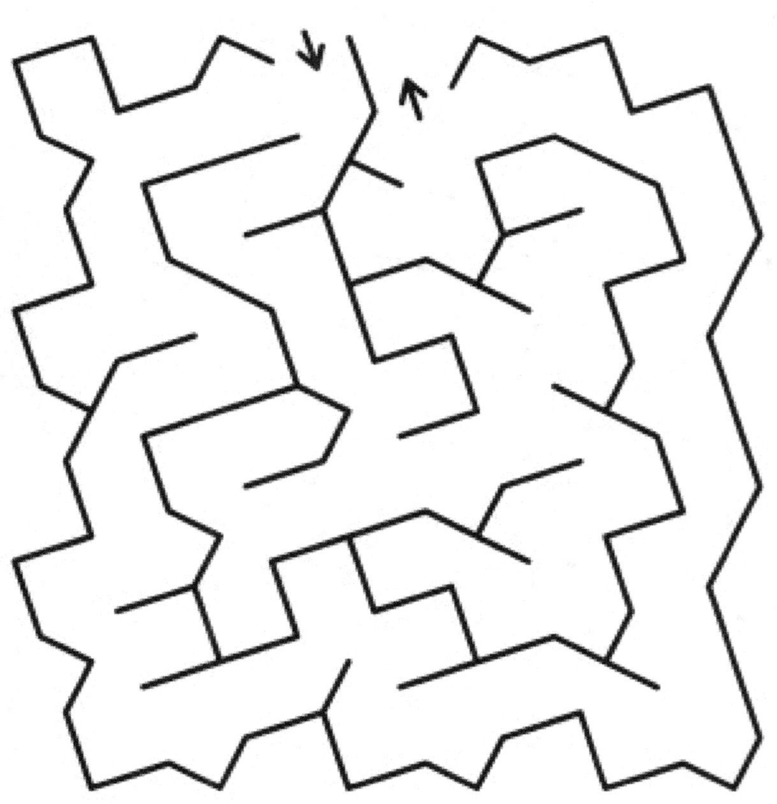

100

Solutions

Solutions

1   2

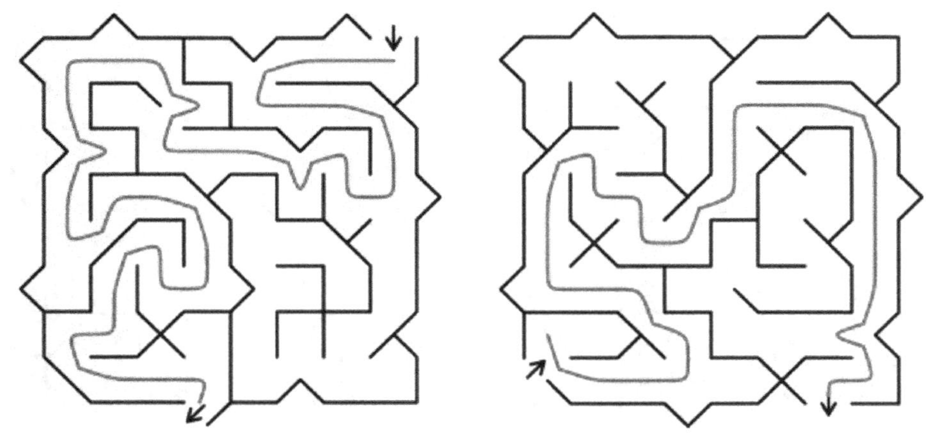

Solutions

3   4

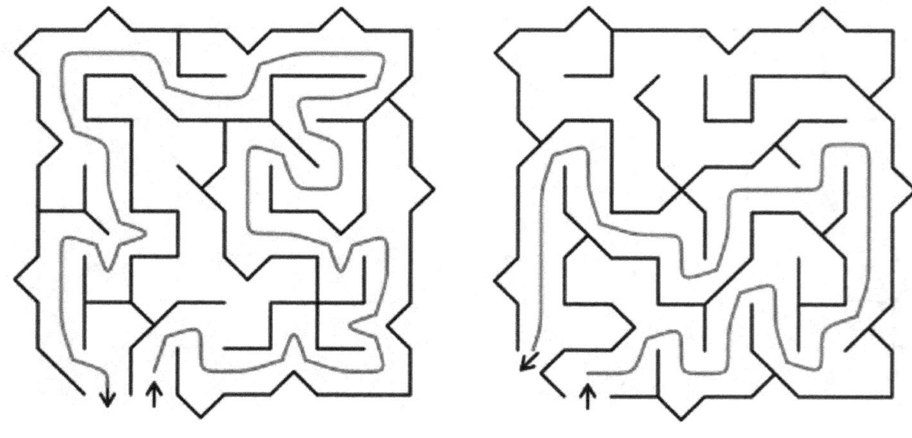

Solutions

5   6

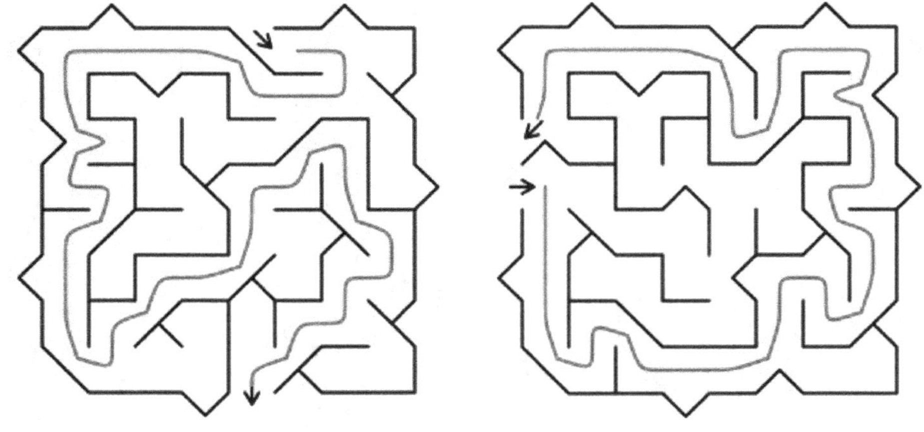

Solutions

7   8

Solutions

9   10

Solutions

11

12

Solutions

13   14

Solutions

15   16

Solutions

17   18

Solutions

19 **20**

Solutions

21   **22**

Solutions

23   24

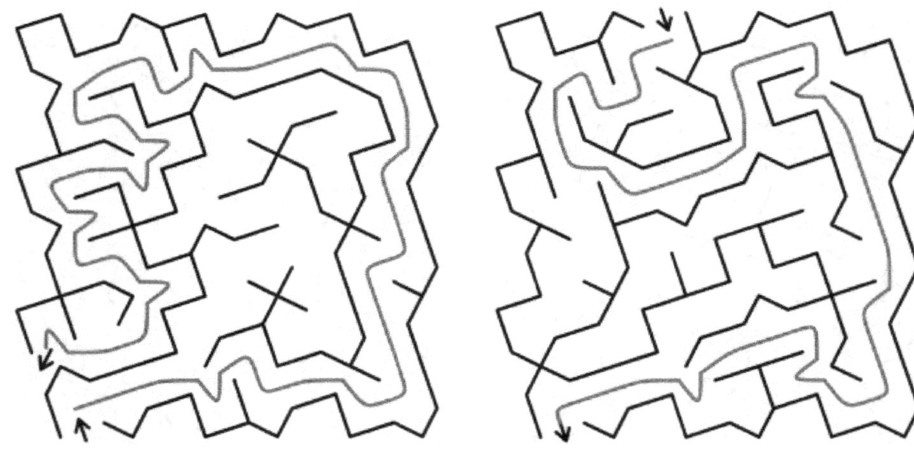

Solutions

25   26

Solutions

27   28

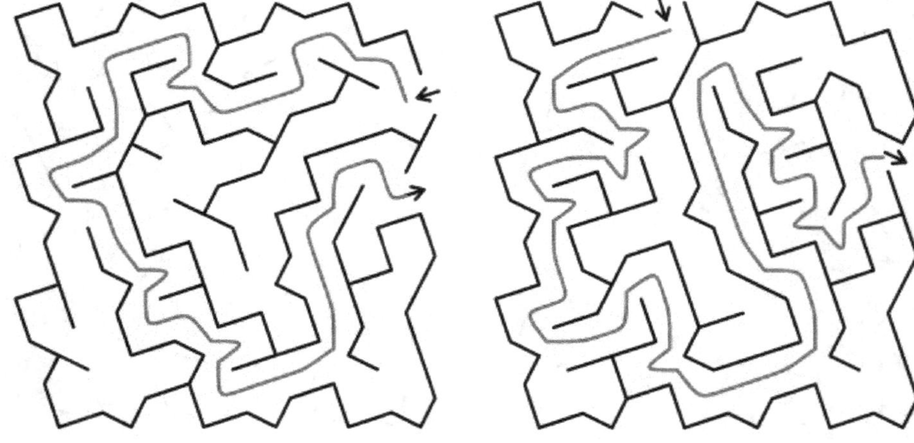

Solutions

29

30

Solutions

31   32

Solutions

33

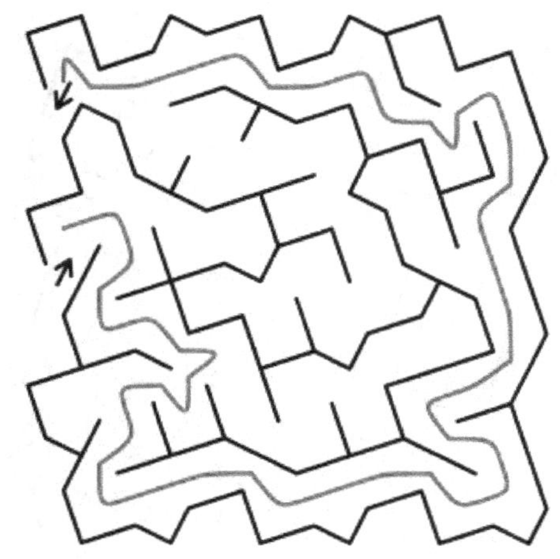

34

Solutions

35   36

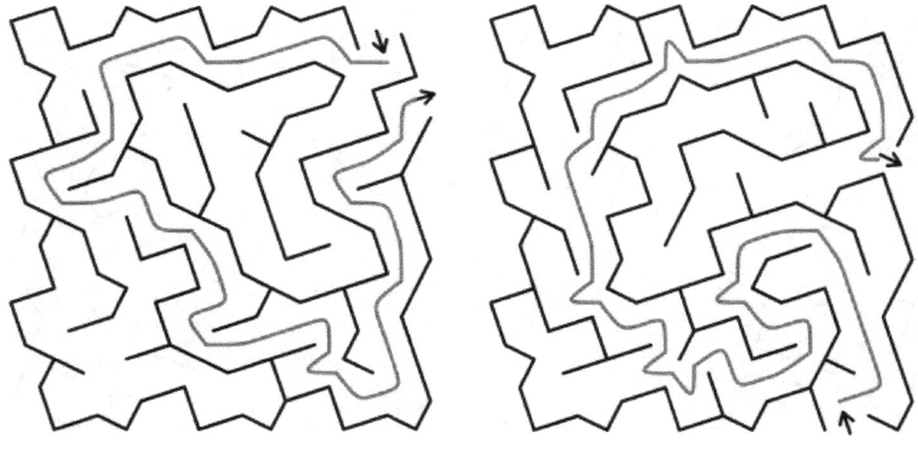

Solutions

37   38

Solutions

39   40

Solutions

41   42

Solutions

43   **44**

Solutions

45　　46

Solutions

47   **48**

Solutions

49

50

Solutions

51   52

Solutions

53   54

Solutions

55   56

Solutions

57   58

Solutions

59   60

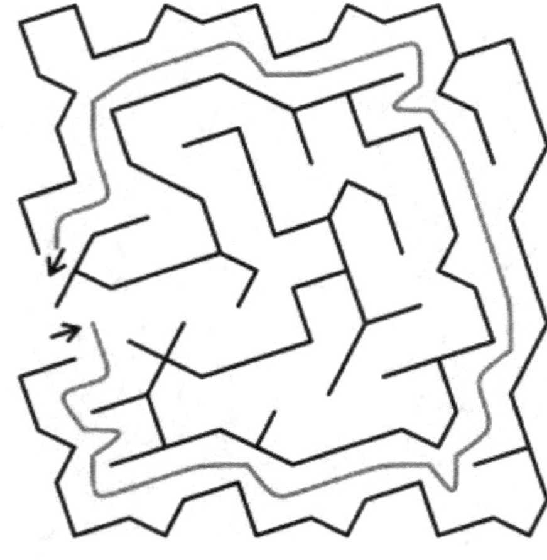

Solutions

61

62

Solutions

63　　　　64

Solutions

65   66

Solutions

67

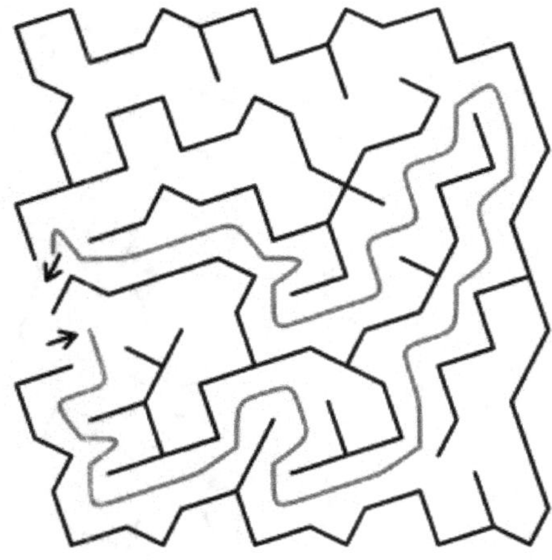

68

Solutions

69   70

Solutions

71 ## 72

Solutions

73   74

Solutions

Solutions

77

78

Solutions

79

80

Solutions

81

82

Solutions

83   84

Solutions

85   86

Solutions

87   88

Solutions

89   90

Solutions

91 92

Solutions

93   94

Solutions

95 96

Solutions

97   98

Solutions

99   100

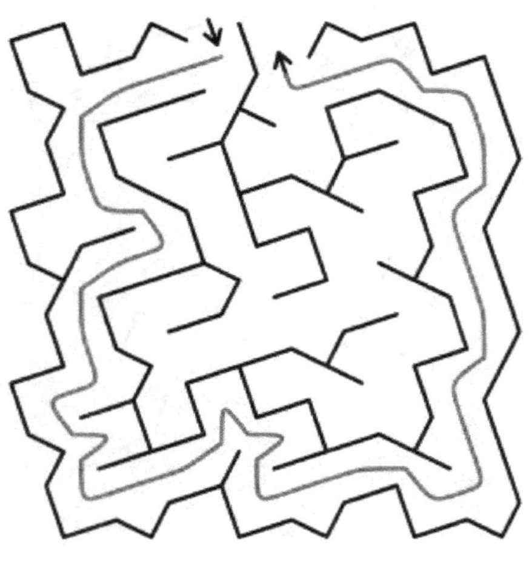